HEINEMANN CHILDREN'S REFERENCE
a division of Heinemann Educational Books Ltd
Halley Court, Jordan Hill, Oxford OX2 8EJ

OXFORD LONDON EDINBURGH
MELBOURNE SYDNEY AUCKLAND
MADRID ATHENS BOLOGNA
SINGAPORE IBADAN NAIROBI HARARE
GABORONE KINGSTON PORTSMOUTH NH(USA)

ISBN 0 431 00325 4

British Library Cataloguing in Publication Data
Bailey, Donna
    We live in Kenya.
    1.   Kenya. Social life
    I.   Title   II. Sproule, Anna   III. Series
    967.6'204

Editorial consultant: Donna Bailey
Designed by Richard Garratt Design
Picture research by Jennifer Garratt

Photographs:
Cover: Stephanie Colasanti FBIPP
Adams Picture Library: 2 (Bertram Davis), 6 (J Grey)
Camerapix Picture Library: title page, 3, 5, 9, 11, 30
Colorific Photo Library: 13 (Tony Carr), 15 (Mary Fisher), 16,
    17 (John Moss), 18 (Terence Spencer), 25 (Mirella
    Ricciardi), 31 (Ben Martin)
Douglas Dickens FRPS: 29
The Hutchison Library: 4 (Liba Taylor), 8 (Timothy Beddow),
    7, 14
OSF Picture Library: 19 (David Shale), 20, 21, 22 (David
    Cayless), 26 (Edwin Sadd), 32 (Mike Birkhead)
Robert Harding Picture Library: 10, 12, 23, 24, 27, 28

Printed in Hong Kong

90 91 92 93 94 95 10 9 8 7 6 5 4 3 2 1

We Live in Kenya

Donna Bailey and Anna Sproule

967

HEINEMANN

Hello! My name is Wanjiru.
I live in Nairobi.
Nairobi is the capital of Kenya.

These trees with purple flowers
grow everywhere in Nairobi.
They are jacaranda trees and give lots of
shade from the hot sun.

We have jacaranda trees in our garden.
There are lots of other flowers too.
We often eat our meals in the garden.
This is my favourite meal, a plate of ugali.
Ugali is a thick porridge made from maize,
which everyone eats with their fingers.

Nairobi is a very busy modern city.
In the centre of the city there are
lots of shops, banks and offices
as well as a big market.

My sister Wangari likes to go to
the market and buy cloth.
She helps Mum make all our dresses.

In the centre of Nairobi there is
a huge statue of Jomo Kenyatta.
He was the first President of Kenya and
head of the government.

Kenyan people like to meet their friends,
and read the newspapers.
They talk about the news and the government.

Every year there is a special parade
in Nairobi on 20 October, Kenyatta Day.
The school children have a holiday and
lots of them go and watch the parade.

Our school choir practises hard
for Kenyatta Day.
We learn special songs to sing when
we march in the parade.

People come from all over Kenya
to join in the parade.
There are lots of bands and groups of
dancers from different parts of the country.

These dancers of the Samburu tribe
are wearing their traditional costume.
They dance the traditional dances
of their tribe.

These drummers are from the Kikuyu tribe.
Many Kikuyu are farmers and live in
the Kenyan highlands, not far from Nairobi.
My family belongs to the Kikuyu tribe.

We often go to visit Dad's relatives
on their farm.
Uncle Njoroge grows coffee on his farm
as well as vegetables and tea.

My aunt helps hoe the vegetables in
the fields to get rid of the weeds.
Kikuyans use a special shaped hoe called
a jembe to separate the weeds
from the vegetables.

My uncle has a very big tractor to
help him plough his fields.
Crops grow well in the Kenyan highlands.

When it is time to pick the tea,
all the women in the village help.
They pick the young tips of the bushes and
put the tea in the baskets on their backs.
The tea leaves are dried and
packed to send to other countries.

Traditional Kikuyu houses are round and
have thatched roofs.
The walls are made of straw and mud bricks
which have been baked in the sun.

The roofs are thatched with grass or reeds.
The thatch keeps the houses cool even in
the hottest weather.

These people are from the Ilchamus tribe.
They live in a fishing village on
the shores of Lake Baringo.

The Ilchamus tribe make a framework of
poles for their houses.
Then they build up the walls and
thatch the roof.

When they have finished, the Ilchamus
often decorate their houses with patterns.

This young girl is from the Masai tribe.
She is wearing lots of bead necklaces.
The Masai make bracelets, necklaces and
belts from beads in different patterns.

The Masai people are not farmers but
herders of cattle.
Their cattle roam the grasslands of
Masai Mara in south-western Kenya.

The young boys herd the cattle.
The Masai move from place to place in
the dry season to find fresh grass
for their cattle to eat.

The women milk the cows and make cheese.
The Masai drink cow's blood mixed with
milk to make them strong.

These men are warriors of the Masai tribe.
They grow their hair very long.
They colour their hair with a red dye called
ochre, then plait it into long thin strands.

Masai warriors are very tall.
They wear bead necklaces and carry
shields and spears.
When they dance together they leap up
high into the air.

Lots of tourists come on holiday
to Kenya to see the animals in
Kenya's famous national parks.
The tourists travel round the parks in
small trucks and vans.

You can see lots of animals
in the national parks.
These monkeys and zebras are in
the Nairobi National Park.

Tourists like taking photographs
of all the wild animals.
This man is taking a photograph
of a rhinoceros.
Rhinos can be dangerous animals, especially
when they get angry and charge at you.

31

There are not many rhinos left in some
of the national parks.
Animal poachers have killed so many
rhinos for their horns that they are now
in danger of dying out.

Index

animals 29, 30, 31
bead necklaces 23, 28
cattle 24, 25
coffee 14
dancers 11, 12, 28
drummers 13
farm 14
government 7, 8
houses 18, 19, 21, 22
Ilchamus 20, 21, 22
jacaranda 3, 4
jembe 15
Kenyan highlands 13, 16
Kenyatta Day 9, 10
Kenyatta, Jomo 7
Kikuyu 13
Lake Baringo 20

market 5, 6
Masai 23, 24, 25, 26, 27, 28
Masai Mara 24
Nairobi 2, 3, 5, 7, 13
national parks 29, 30, 32
parade 9, 10, 11
poachers 32
rhinoceros 31, 32
roofs 18, 19, 21
Samburu 12
tea 14
tourists 29, 31
tractor 16
ugali 4
vegetables 14, 15
walls 18, 21
warriors 27, 28